EXPLORATION FOR KIDS

THE AMERICAS, COLUMBUS, PONCE DE LEON AND MORE

EXPLORING AMERICAN HISTORY
3RD GRADE SOCIAL STUDIES

BABY PROFESSOR
EDUCATION KIDS

Speedy Publishing LLC

40 E. Main St. #1156

Newark, DE 19711

www.speedypublishing.com

Copyright 2017

In this book, we're going to talk about some of the first European explorers who came to the Americas. So, let's get right to it!

WHO REALLY DISCOVERED AMERICA?

Many people believe that Christopher Columbus discovered America in 1492. However, there are many other theories regarding which Europeans came to America first. Some of these theories have a basis in historical fact and others may only be legends.

Landing of Columbus

Saint Brendan and his monks set sail for a western land

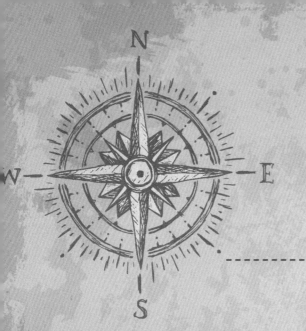

SAINT BRENDAN AND HIS CURRACH

There's a legend that as early as the 6th century, an Irish monk by the name of Saint Brendan traveled across the Atlantic Ocean to North America. His boat, called a currach, was built out of wood and animal skins.

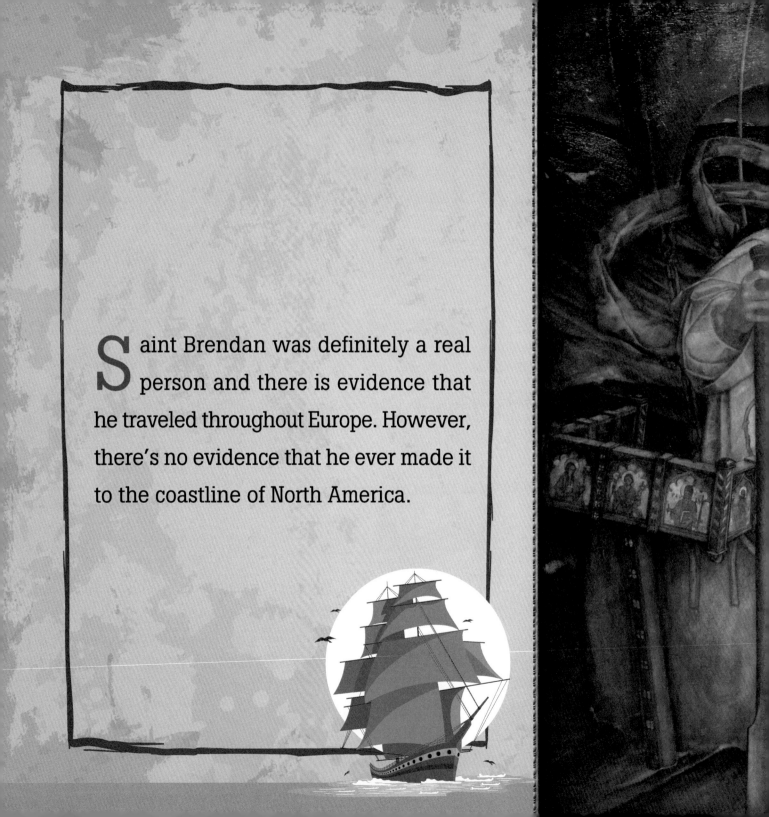

Saint Brendan was definitely a real person and there is evidence that he traveled throughout Europe. However, there's no evidence that he ever made it to the coastline of North America.

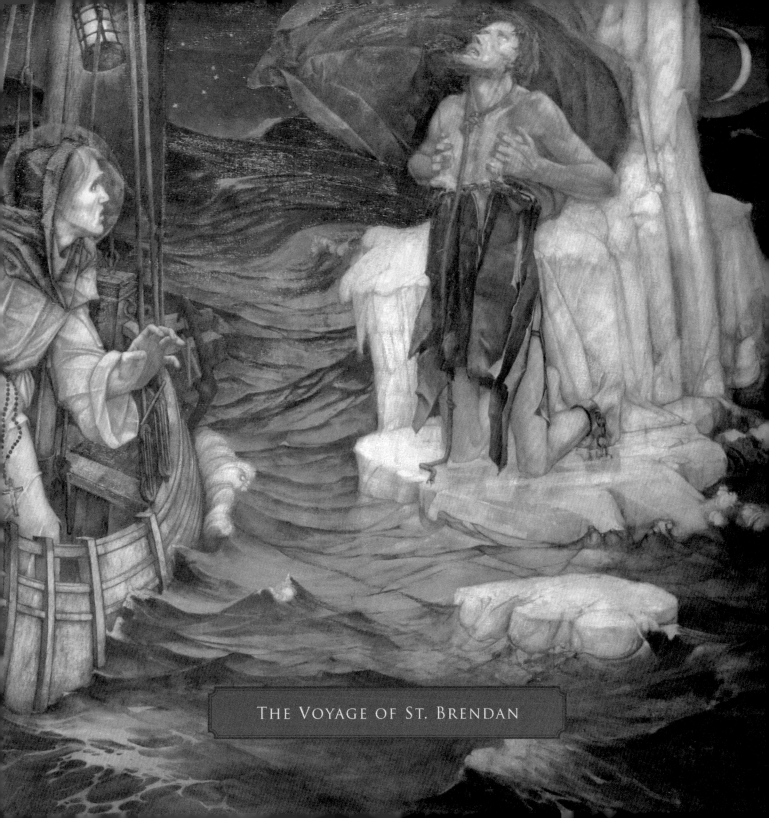

THE VOYAGE OF ST. BRENDAN

It seems hardly possible that anyone could travel that far in such a simply constructed boat, but in 1976, Tim Severin, a writer who was curious about the legend,

ST. BRENDANAN THE NAVIGATOR

constructed a replica of Saint Brendan's boat and sailed it based on ancient records written by monks in Ireland. He proved it could be done when he landed in Canada.

THE VIKINGS

Circa 1000 AD, a Viking by the name of Leif Erikson, traveled to North America from Greenland on a Viking ship and landed in what is now known as Newfoundland, a province of Canada. Leif was the son of a famous Viking known as Erik the Red. He named the land "Vinland," which means land of wine.

Vikings Heading for Land

Vikings discovered VINLAND (now NEWFOUNDLAND)

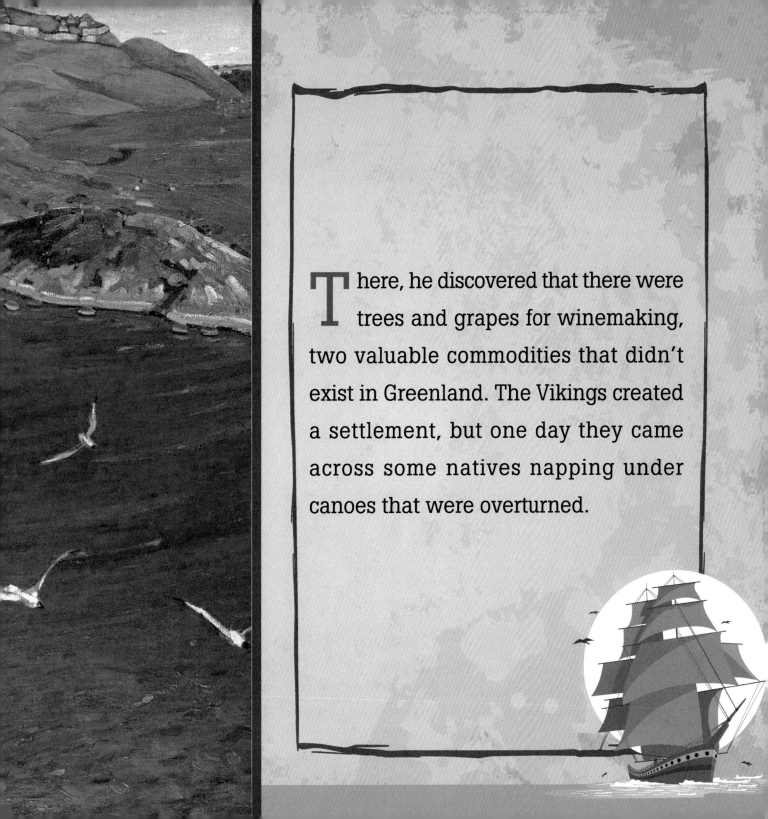

There, he discovered that there were trees and grapes for winemaking, two valuable commodities that didn't exist in Greenland. The Vikings created a settlement, but one day they came across some natives napping under canoes that were overturned.

The Vikings killed these Native Americans so their relationship got off to a violent start. There was some attempt to trade goods that each group needed,

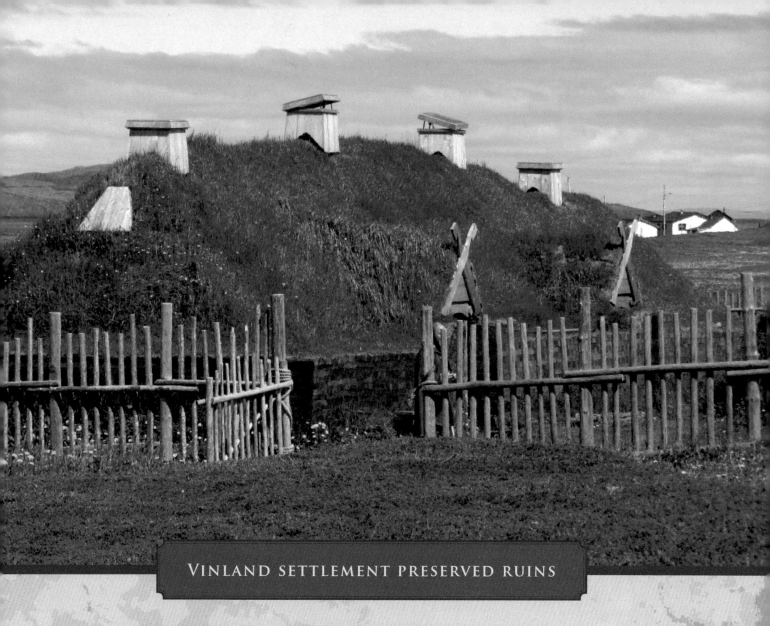

VINLAND SETTLEMENT PRESERVED RUINS

but the Vikings were outnumbered so most of them only stayed in their Vinland settlement for a couple of years before they went back to Greenland.

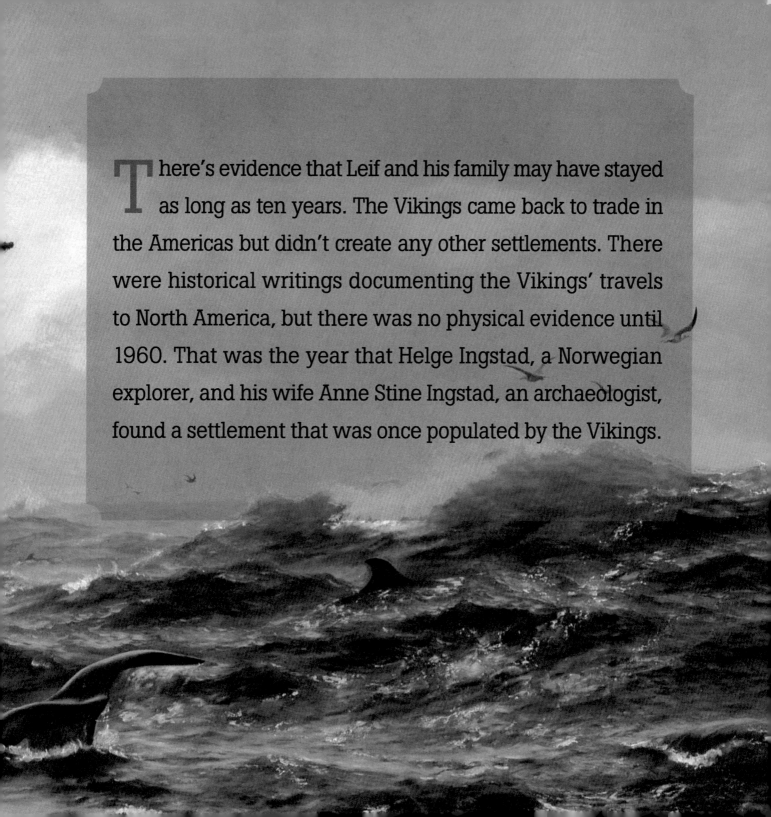

There's evidence that Leif and his family may have stayed as long as ten years. The Vikings came back to trade in the Americas but didn't create any other settlements. There were historical writings documenting the Vikings' travels to North America, but there was no physical evidence until 1960. That was the year that Helge Ingstad, a Norwegian explorer, and his wife Anne Stine Ingstad, an archaeologist, found a settlement that was once populated by the Vikings.

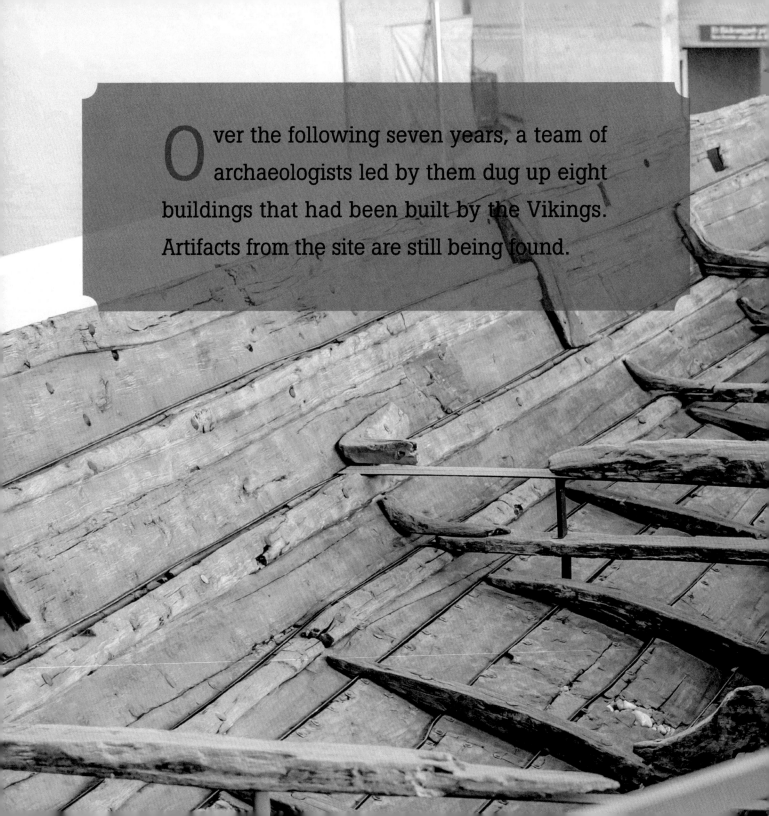

Over the following seven years, a team of archaeologists led by them dug up eight buildings that had been built by the Vikings. Artifacts from the site are still being found.

THE NATIVE PEOPLE

In many ways it doesn't make sense to talk about Europeans "discovering" the Americas. After all, it's not as if there were no people in North or South America when they arrived. There were millions of native peoples on both continents.

Their ancestors had discovered the Americas thousands of years before. Although these groups were all very different from each other, they all had ceremonial rituals honoring the stories of their ancient ancestors.

CHRISTOPHER COLUMBUS

THE STORY OF CHRISTOPHER COLUMBUS

Christopher Columbus was an educated man. He was Italian, but he had worked in the country of Portugal for many years. He had been a sailor and had traveled to Iceland as well as Africa. He had also been a mapmaker and a bookseller.

He believed the world was a sphere and not flat. The silks and spices of the Far East were coveted by Europeans.

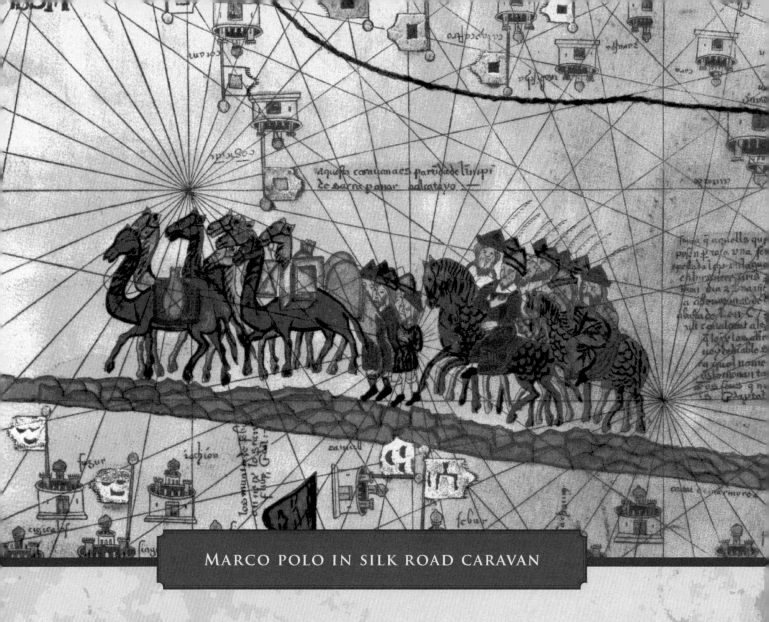

MARCO POLO IN SILK ROAD CARAVAN

T o get these valuable items, European traders traveled over treacherous deserts and high, mountain peaks along the famous Silk Road, where Marco Polo had walked two centuries before.

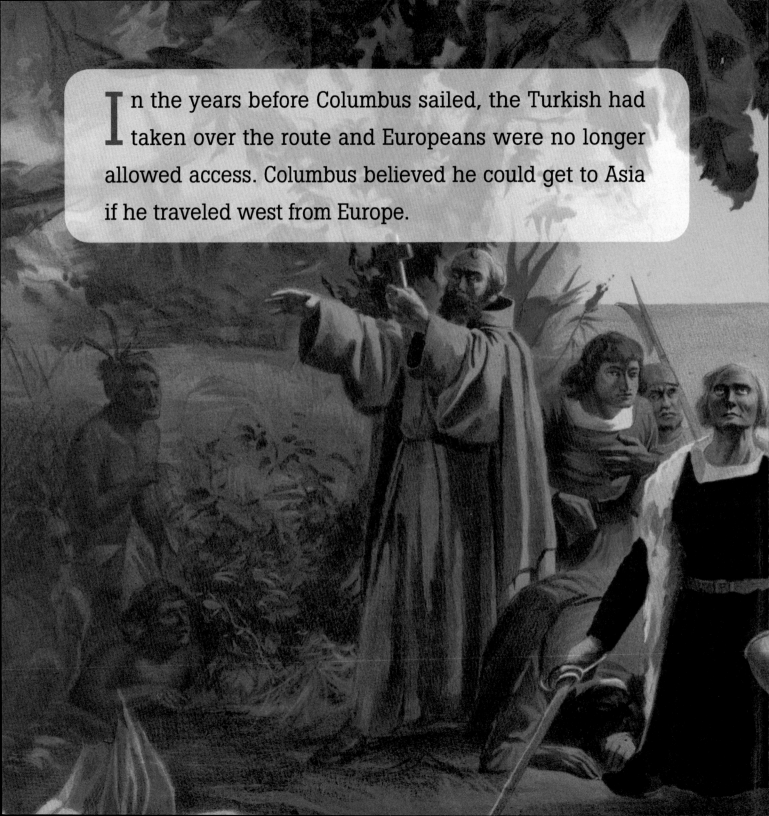

In the years before Columbus sailed, the Turkish had taken over the route and Europeans were no longer allowed access. Columbus believed he could get to Asia if he traveled west from Europe.

He had a book in his possession that was written by a French author, Pierre d'Ailly. The book was called "Imago Mundi," which translates to "Image of the World."

In this book, the author made a case that the "Ocean Sea" wasn't as big as it seemed and that it might be possible to cross it within a few days.

KING OF PORTUGAL

Columbus brought a bold plan to the king of Portugal, King John II. Portuguese explorers were making progress on their exploration of Africa and gaining territory and new trade routes. King John II gave the plan to his legion of astronomers and mapmakers. They came to the conclusion that the East was too far away to be reached by the route Columbus had proposed.

Even though Columbus had been rejected by the king of Portugal, he decided to try again in Spain, a country where he'd never been. Armed with a letter of introduction, he visited King Ferdinand and his wife, Queen Isabella. They also submitted his plan for review and got the same response. They rejected him twice and after six years of waiting for them to say yes, he threatened to offer the same plan to the King of France.

King Ferdinand and Queen Isabella

He was on his way, riding on a mule on a dusty road, when King Ferdinand's court advisors prevailed upon the king. If Columbus offered the plan to France and they were successful, Spain would be shamed. The advisers suggested that the king and queen let Columbus risk his life and if he brought back riches they would belong to Spain and help Spain become more powerful.

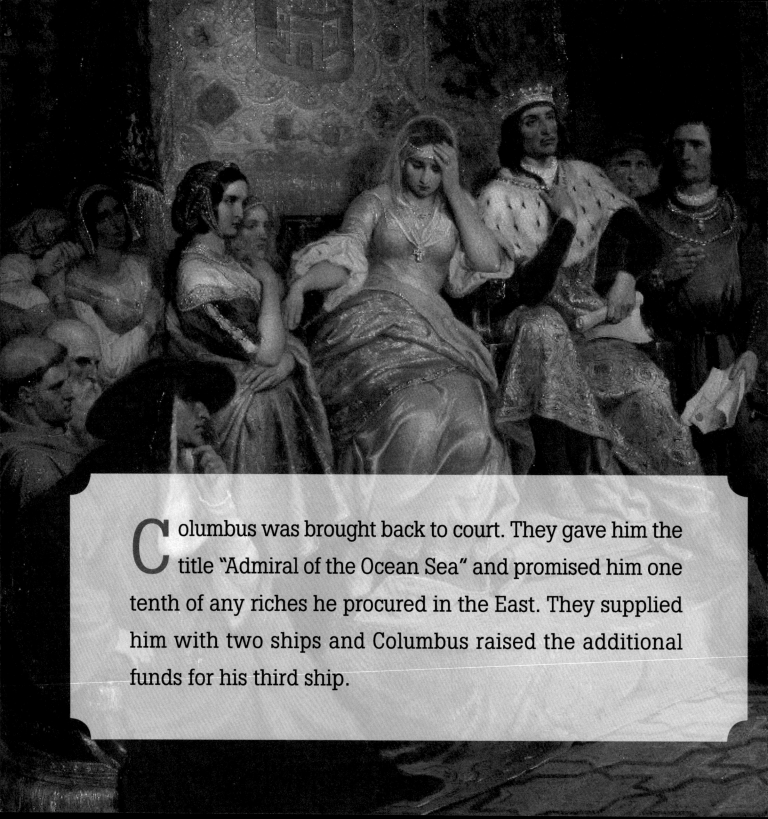

Columbus was brought back to court. They gave him the title "Admiral of the Ocean Sea" and promised him one tenth of any riches he procured in the East. They supplied him with two ships and Columbus raised the additional funds for his third ship.

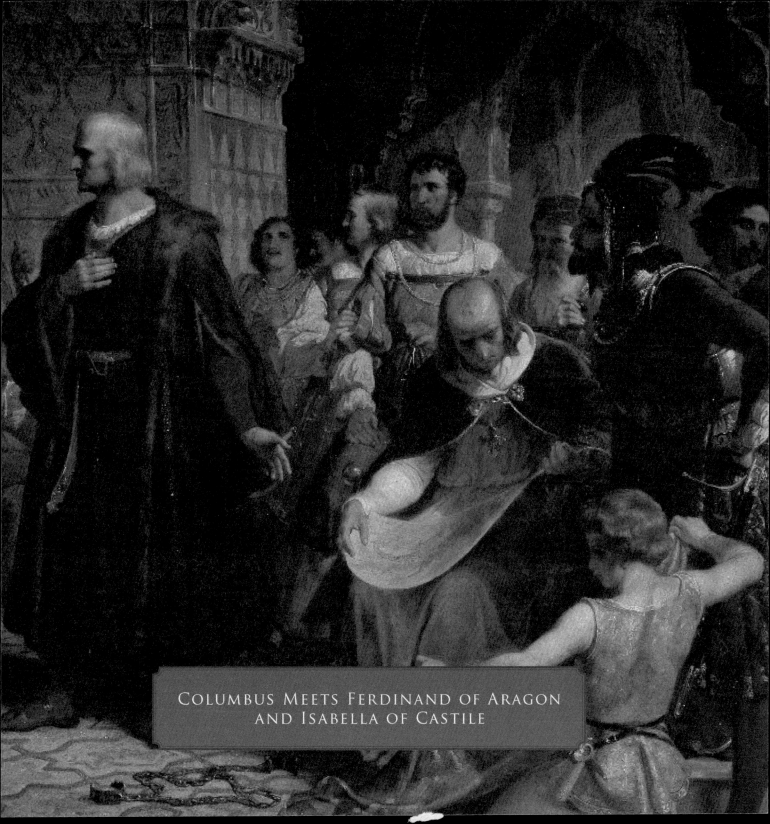

Columbus Meets Ferdinand of Aragon
and Isabella of Castile

Columbus taking possession

In August of 1492, he set sail with his crew of Spanish sailors on the Niña, the Pinta, and the Santa Maria. The journey was incredibly difficult. At one point, the Spanish crew members threatened to throw their admiral off the ship. They didn't trust Columbus because he wasn't Spanish. They were terrified that they hadn't found land and that sea monsters would rise from the sea and devour them. The situation got so bad that Columbus kept the true record of the amount of time it was taking them in a second journal so it wouldn't be revealed to the crew. He managed to calm them down and on October 12, 1492, land was spotted.

They had landed on a tiny island in what is known today as the Bahamas. Columbus named the island "San Salvador."

He called the local natives living there "Indians" because he thought he had reached the country of India.

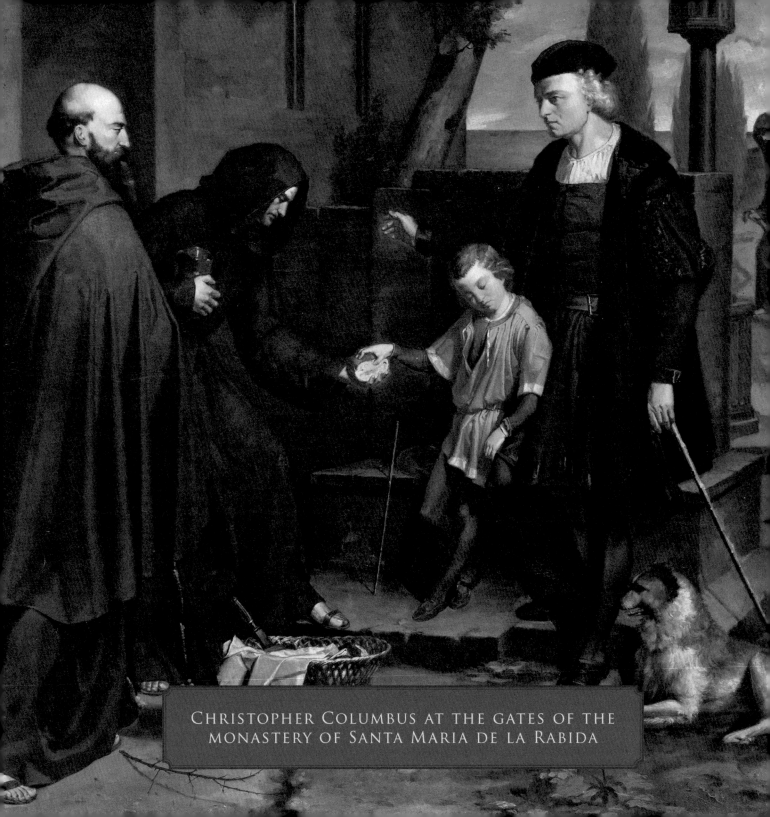

Christopher Columbus at the gates of the monastery of Santa Maria de la Rabida

The people he had found there were actually the Tainos, a group of gentle people who welcomed Columbus. Columbus returned to Spain a hero and he made three later trips to what are now known as the Caribbean Islands as well as an island known today as Hispaniola. He also made trips along the coasts of Central and South America. Although he didn't realize he had discovered a "New World," he started a historic time period of European expansion.

WHO WAS PONCE DE LEON?

Juan Ponce de Leon was a soldier who fought against the Moors during the rule of King Ferdinand and Queen Isabella. The Spanish defeated the Moors and once again had control of the Iberian Peninsula. After the war ended, Ponce de Leon was seeking a new challenge. He traveled with Columbus on his second trip to the "New World." Eventually, he was appointed governor of a settlement on the island of Hispaniola. He became a rich man from farming and shipping produce back to Spain for sale.

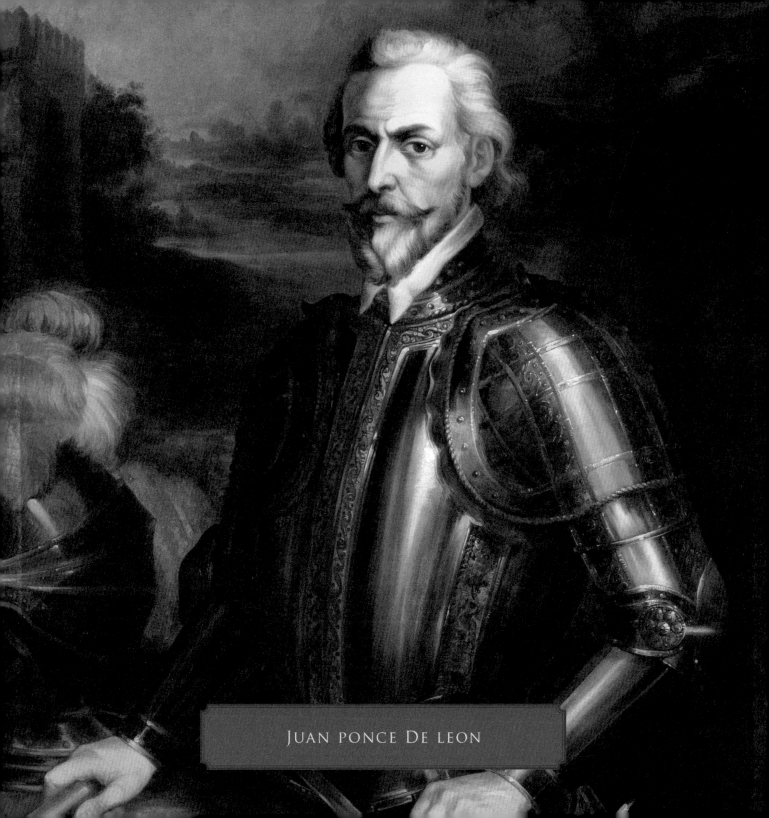
JUAN PONCE DE LEON

Seeking yet another new adventure, Ponce de Leon went off to explore new areas and in 1506 he traveled to Puerto Rico where he found fertile land as well as gold. With the king's approval, he began a settlement on the island and became its first governor. The Tainos who lived there were forced to work on farms and in the mines to obtain gold for the Spanish.

Many of them died because the Spaniards treated them cruelly and because of diseases, such as smallpox, which the Europeans brought with them. Due to political reasons, Ponce de Leon lost his position as governor of Puerto Rico, but the king wanted to reward him for his loyal service so he funded another expedition. In 1513, Ponce de Leon headed north of Puerto Rico accompanied by 200 crew members on three ships.

SEPTEMTRIO.

Naguater.

Chiacha

Canaragay.

Tali.

Cofle

Nisoona

Vlibahaly.

Guax uli.

Xuala.

Chalaqu

Chague.

Xuaquile.

Lacane.

Chillano.

Quigata

Tafcalifa.

Cafaqui

Caritacheque

Ayx.

Achufi.

Aym

Xualatino.

Rio del Spirito Santo

Culuta

Rio de Cañaueral

Rio de Flores

Rio de Nieues

P. de S. Marita

Bayabaxa

Baya de S. Iofeph.

Rio Seco

OCCIDENS.

C. de Cruz.

C. Defierro

Montañas

Rio del Oro

Rio de Pesca dores.

Cofta Bara

Rio Escondido.

Medanos della Mag dalena.

Rio de las Palmas

LA FLORIDA.

Auctore Hieron. Chiaues.

Circulus

Cancri.

Tortug

In April of that same year, they spotted land, which they believed was another island. Eventually, they realized it was a much larger piece of land than they had originally believed. Ponce de Leon named the land "Florida" after the Festival of Flowers since they had discovered it around the Easter holiday.

IN CONCLUSION..

No one knows who the very first people who set foot in North and South America were. The native peoples who lived there when the Europeans arrived had been there for thousands of years. The Vikings may have been the first non-native people to set foot in North America around 1000 AD.

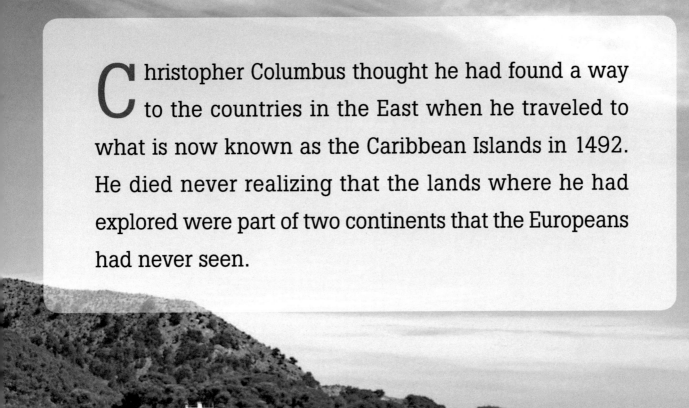

Christopher Columbus thought he had found a way to the countries in the East when he traveled to what is now known as the Caribbean Islands in 1492. He died never realizing that the lands where he had explored were part of two continents that the Europeans had never seen.

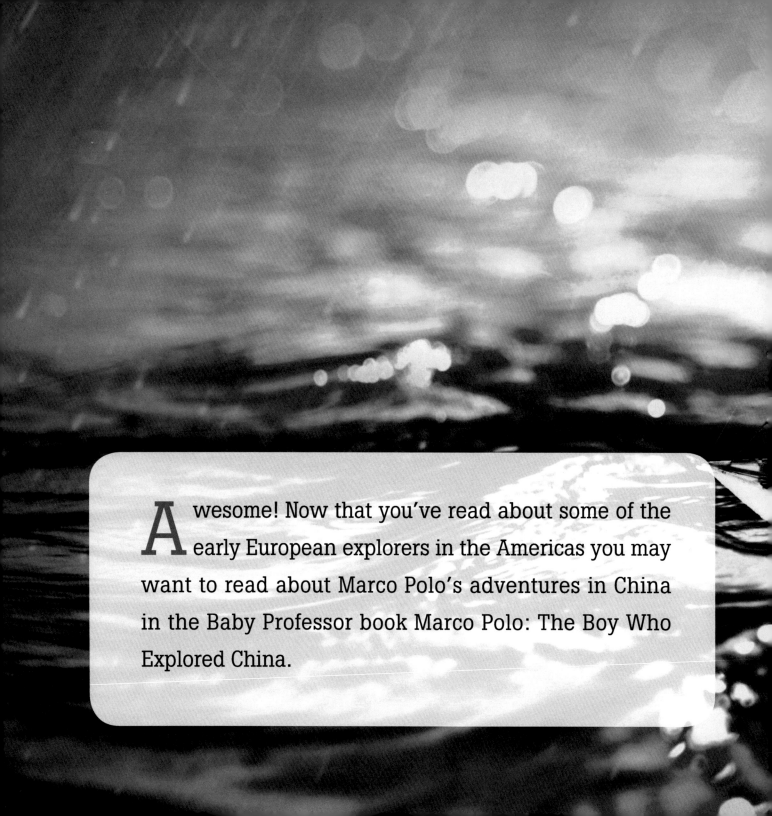

Awesome! Now that you've read about some of the early European explorers in the Americas you may want to read about Marco Polo's adventures in China in the Baby Professor book Marco Polo: The Boy Who Explored China.

Visit

BABY PROFESSOR
EDUCATION KIDS

www.BabyProfessorBooks.com

to download Free Baby Professor eBooks
and view our catalog of new and exciting
Children's Books

Made in the USA
Middletown, DE
31 July 2018